Roosevelt's Rough Riders

by Andrew Santella

Content Adviser: Lewis L. Gould, Professor Emeritus,
Department of History,
University of Texas at Austin

Reading Adviser: Rosemary G. Palmer, Ph.D.,
Department of Literacy, College of Education,
Boise State University

COMPASS POINT BOOKS
MINNEAPOLIS, MINNESOTA

Compass Point Books
3109 West 50th Street, #115
Minneapolis, MN 55410

Visit Compass Point Books on the Internet at *www.compasspointbooks.com*
or e-mail your request to *custserv@compasspointbooks.com*

On the cover: Roosevelt and the Rough Riders

Photographs ©:
Corbis, cover, 16, 18, 21, 22, 31, 39; Prints Old & Rare, back cover (far left); Library of Congress,
back cover, 19, 26, 32, 40 (all); Bettmann/Corbis, 4, 12, 17; DVIC/NARA, 5, 11, 37, 38; Hulton
Archive/Getty Images, 7; Underwood & Underwood/Corbis, 9, 25; Stock Montage, 13, 34; MPI/Getty
Images, 14; Theodore Roosevelt Collection, Harvard College Library, 15; North Wind Picture Archives,
23, 24, 27, 28, 29, 30, 41; Courtesy Frederic Remington Art Museum, Ogdensburg, New York, 35;
The Granger Collection, New York, 36.

Editor: Sue Vander Hook
Designer/Page Production: Bradfordesign, Inc./Les Tranby
Photo Researcher: Svetlana Zhurkin
Cartographer: XNR Productions, Inc.
Educational Consultant: Diane Smolinski
Library Consultant: Kathleen Baxter

Managing Editor: Catherine Neitge
Creative Director: Keith Griffin
Editorial Director: Carol Jones

Library of Congress Cataloging-in-Publication Data
Santella, Andrew.
  Roosevelt's Rough Riders / by Andrew Santella.
    p. cm.–(We the people)
  Includes bibliographical references and index.
  ISBN 0-7565-1268-9 (hardcover)
  ISBN 0-7565-1732-X (paperback)
1. United States. Army. Volunteer Cavalry, 1st—History—Juvenile literature. 2. Roosevelt, Theodore,
1858-1919—Juvenile literature. 3. Spanish-American War, 1898—Regimental histories—Juvenile literature.
4. Spanish-American War, 1898—Cuba—Juvenile literature. I. Title. II. Series: We the people (Series)
(Compass Point Books)
  E725.451st .S26 2006
  973.8'942'097291—dc22   2005002468

TABLE OF CONTENTS

THE ROUGH RIDERS

He wore little round eyeglasses. His bushy mustache sometimes covered up his toothy grin. Around his neck was a blue and white polka-dot handkerchief. Sitting tall on his horse, he sported a floppy felt hat and leather gloves up to his elbows. Colonel Theodore Roosevelt was hard to miss.

Theodore Roosevelt trained the Rough Riders to fight on horseback.

He was not an average soldier. Even his speaking voice was special. It was loud, clear, and high-pitched—a voice his troops recognized and obeyed.

Roosevelt's troops were special, too. About 1,000 men made up the unique regiment of volunteers known as the 1st United States Volunteer Cavalry. Some were rugged cowboys from the West; others were college graduates

The Rough Riders raised the U.S. flag on San Juan Hill, Cuba, after their victory.

from the East. But they had several things in common. They could ride a horse and shoot a gun. They also wanted to fight under Roosevelt's leadership. That's why they lined up by the hundreds to volunteer.

As part of the U.S. Army, this regiment was sent to Cuba to fight in the Spanish-American War. On July 1, 1898, Roosevelt led these rough and reckless soldiers into battle. Their assignment was to attack Spanish forces positioned high on two hills. The unit made its way up the first hill. Bullets flew and cannon shells exploded around them. Yet they pushed the Spanish back and took control of the hill. Roosevelt assembled his men for a second charge. He hoped this one would win the battle.

"Follow me, boys!" he shouted. He charged forward toward Spanish lines. Roosevelt went only a short distance when he looked back. His troops were not following him. He was nearly alone in the open field, facing Spanish gunfire by himself. He raced back, angry and embarrassed, and demanded to know why they hadn't followed him.

American troops charged up San Juan Hill in Cuba on
July 1, 1898, during the Spanish-American War.

"Sorry, colonel, we didn't hear you," one of them replied. Try again, they said, and we'll be right behind you. The regiment followed Roosevelt this time. Their successful advance up San Juan Hill became a key victory in the war.

Back in the United States, Roosevelt and his volunteer soldiers were hailed as heroes. Newspaper stories called the battle "Teddie's charge up San Juan Hill." Reporters dubbed these rough-and-tough soldiers Roosevelt's Rough Riders. Their fame spread across the country. The victory in Cuba took their fearless leader all the way to the White House.

A RISING POWER

Spain's defeat in Cuba made the fading Spanish empire
even weaker. Cuba was part of what was once a vast
Spanish territory. In the 1490s, Spain started acquiring
land. When Christopher Columbus set sail in 1492, Spain

The Spanish army stands in front of the Palace Colonnade, Havana, Cuba, in 1898.

In 1898, Spain ruled Cuba and Puerto Rico.

became the first European nation to establish colonies in the Western Hemisphere. But by the end of the 1800s, Spain had lost most of its empire.

While Spain was weakening, the United States was growing more powerful. In the 1890s, some Americans still believed in the 50-year-old idea of manifest destiny. They wanted to expand beyond U.S. borders. Many people hoped to plant the U.S. flag in Cuba. Others wanted Cuba to be free and independent.

Cubans wanted their independence from Spain. For more than 20 years, Cuban rebels had been fighting for freedom. If Spain could not defeat the rebels, the U.S. government thought Cuba should be free. This conflict set the stage for a disaster that pushed the United States to the brink of war with Spain.

The battleship USS *Maine* arrived in Cuba in January 1898. It docked in Havana Harbor to protect American citizens

The battleship Maine *enters Havana Harbor, Cuba, in 1898.*

living there. On February 15, a gigantic explosion destroyed the huge vessel. The twisted remains sank to the bottom of the harbor. More than 260 Americans died that day in the blast.

Investigators for the U.S. Navy declared that an underwater mine caused the explosion. Later

Some seamen at the back of the ship survived the explosion of the Maine.

investigations showed the explosion might have been inside the ship. But many Americans were sure Spain was to blame. They cried out for war. "Remember the *Maine*!" became their rallying cry.

U.S. President William McKinley tried to solve the problem, but tension between the United States and Spain was too great. On April 21, 1898, the United States officially declared war on Spain. The Spanish-American War had begun.

Front page of the New York Journal, *February 17, 1898*

ROOSEVELT GOES TO WAR

The United States rushed to prepare itself for war.
Volunteers by the thousands came forward to join the fight.
No volunteer was more eager than 40-year-old Theodore
Roosevelt. He was determined to be involved in some
action and prove his manhood by fighting in a war. From

*Theodore Roosevelt (1858-1919) visited the Badlands of
South Dakota in 1885, after the death of his first wife.*

the time he was a young boy in New York City, he had wanted to make himself stronger. His father had commanded him, "Build your body," and Roosevelt obeyed.

Theodore "Teddy" Roosevelt at the age of 4

He taught himself to box and ride horses. He came to believe in the healing power of an active life. After the death of his first wife, Roosevelt moved to the West. In the Dakota Territory, he ran a cattle ranch. Life on the ranch was not much like the sophisticated world he knew in New York City. But Roosevelt came to love the West and his life on the back of a horse. His friends were cowboys and ranch hands. He learned to drive cattle

15

Roosevelt, dressed in buckskins, lived on a North Dakota ranch from 1884-1886.

and went on hunting expeditions in the wilds of Wyoming.

After some time, Roosevelt returned to the East. He worked in the federal government and then served as New York City police commissioner. In 1897, President McKinley appointed him assistant secretary of the Navy. In his new job, Roosevelt urged the United States to prepare for war with Spain. When the war came, he believed he had to share in the fighting. He resigned from his position as secretary of the Navy and volunteered to fight.

Roosevelt served as assistant secretary of the U.S. Navy from 1896-1898.

In 1898, the U.S. Army had only 28,000 soldiers. It needed at least 75,000 troops to fight the large Spanish army in Cuba. Congress approved the formation of volunteer regiments to help the regular Army. Russell Alger, secretary of war, offered Roosevelt the command of a volunteer unit—the 1st United States Volunteer Cavalry. Volunteers would be chosen from Arizona, New Mexico, Oklahoma, and other parts of the West.

Roosevelt was delighted with the offer, but he had doubts about leading the regiment. He had never served in the military, and he wondered if he knew enough to command the unit. So he suggested his longtime friend, Leonard Wood, for the position. Wood had the military experience Roosevelt lacked. Alger gave Wood leadership of the regiment. Roosevelt was second in command.

Leonard Wood (1860-1927), a doctor and Army officer, was the first leader of the Rough Riders.

AN UNUSUAL GROUP

With the famous Theodore Roosevelt recruiting volunteers, men poured in from the West. Many were cowboys and ranch hands who made their living on

A Choctaw Indian Rough Rider

19

horseback. Volunteers included Native Americans from reservations. One recruit was William "Little Billy" McGinty. He was an expert broncobuster, who could tame and train the wildest horses. Roosevelt said McGinty "never had walked a hundred yards if by any possibility he could ride."

The regiment was supposed to have 800 volunteers. Soon, the U.S. War Department increased the size to 1,000. To fill the extra positions, Wood and Roosevelt began accepting volunteers from the East. Many of them shared Roosevelt's background. They came from wealthy families and outstanding colleges like Harvard. They included polo players, football players, tennis champions, clergymen, and policemen. There were miners from tough Arizona boomtowns and lawyers from big cities. Some were ranch hands, bakers, doctors, and sheriffs. People began calling this unusual group the Rough Riders.

Applicants were tested for their physical strength.

They also had to be able to ride a spirited horse and shoot a gun. There were many more qualified men than Roosevelt and Wood needed. They found it difficult to turn any of them away. Finally, volunteers were chosen.

These millionaires from New York joined the Rough Riders.

Rough Rider Captain William "Buckey" O'Neill on horseback

One of the officers was Buckey O'Neill, a sheriff from the tough Arizona mining territory. He became good friends with Dr. James Robert Church, a surgeon who had been educated at Princeton University. The regiment's first trumpeter was a Native American. The second trumpeter was Emilio Cassi, an immigrant from the small country of Monaco.

The Rough Riders assembled for training at Camp

Wood near San Antonio, Texas. Already in good physical shape, these volunteers quickly got ready for war. Armed with rifles, revolvers, and their own guns, they practiced shooting every day. Each man was given a horse to ride and train.

Their uniforms matched their rugged personalities. They wore blue flannel shirts, brown pants, leggings, boots, and slouch hats. Around their necks were loosely knotted handkerchiefs.

Roosevelt in his Rough Rider uniform

Roosevelt was delighted with the Rough Riders. "It is as typical an American regiment as ever

Rough Riders shoe a bronco at Camp Wood near San Antonio, Texas.

marched or fought," he wrote a friend. They began each day with drills, first on foot and then on horseback. The horses were as wild as most of the soldiers. Each man taught his steed to stay in line and obey his commands. Roosevelt trained his troops to use their horses as their first weapon. He wrote, "[I]f my men could be trained to hit their adversaries with their horses, it was a matter of small amount whether ... sabres, lances, or revolvers were used."

At the end of each day, the Rough Riders cooked and washed dishes. They all worked together, rich and poor, businessmen and outlaws, Indians and former Indian fighters.

A Rough Rider kneads dough for bread at Camp Wood.

25

ON TO CUBA

Their training was completed quickly, and the Rough
Riders were ready for action. They loaded their equipment
onto the train that would take them to Tampa, Florida.
Saddles, bridles, and luggage went in baggage cars. The

Rough Riders arrive by train in Tampa, Florida, to prepare to sail to Cuba.

26

horses traveled in cattle cars. At every train stop, people cheered for the Rough Riders and waved the U.S. flag.

When they arrived in Tampa, their excitement was high. Soon they would board ships bound for Cuba, just 500 miles (800 kilometers) away. But some of the Rough Riders were in for a bitter disappointment. Room aboard

Rough Riders wait on the dock at Port Tampa, Florida, to board ships for Cuba. **27**

the ships was limited, so about 400 of them had to stay in Tampa. Trooper Frank Brito remembered his disbelief at being left behind. "We had come a long way together and being left out at the last moment was not something any of us had counted on." Then they learned there was not enough room for all their horses. They had been trained on

horseback, and now most of them would have to fight on foot. Finally, the soldiers boarded the crowded ships. But the ships didn't move out of the harbor. Rumor was that Spanish ships were lurking in the high seas. The trip to Cuba would be delayed until the route was safe.

Soldiers onboard the Yucatan *wait to set sail for Cuba.*

28

The Rough Riders row to shore at Daiquiri, Cuba.

A week went by, and finally the ships set sail. For six days, the soldiers endured awful conditions onboard. The heat was unbearable. They drank unclean water and ate canned beef that often was rotten. Many of the Rough Riders were sick during the entire trip.

Their landing was even more difficult than their voyage. The ships didn't have enough small boats, so many men had to swim to shore. The sea was rough, and at least two soldiers drowned. The horses were put overboard and expected to swim. Some of them drowned, too. Most of the troops made it to shore and prepared for battle.

THE FIRST BATTLE

The Rough Riders and regular Army regiments soon were ordered to begin marching inland. Their goal was to reach Santiago de Cuba, the second-largest city on the island.

Scene at Daiquiri, Cuba, the day the Army landed

Troop D of the Rough Riders lines up as they wait to march inland into Cuba.

A large Spanish force was there, and so was the Spanish naval fleet. The Rough Riders were used to riding horses, not marching. The heat was wearing them out. They got rid of their backpacks and some supplies to make their load lighter.

On June 24, 1898, at a place called Las Guásimas, they came upon a group of Spanish soldiers hiding in trenches. The Rough Riders came under heavy fire. Fighting alongside them were the Buffalo Soldiers, African-American troops of the 9th and 10th cavalries. The Rough Riders and the Buffalo

Buffalo Soldiers was a name given to African-American U.S. Army regiments commissioned in 1866 to patrol the West after the Civil War.

Soldiers fired on the Spanish forces and moved forward. Outnumbered, the Spanish retreated.

This first battle was costly. Sixteen U.S. soldiers were killed; eight of them were Rough Riders. The next day, the regiment buried all their dead in one common grave.

Roosevelt observed, "There could be no more honorable burial than that of these men in a common grave—Indian and cowboy, miner, packer and college athlete." After the battle, Roosevelt was made colonel and given full command of the Rough Riders.

THE CHARGE UP
SAN JUAN HILL

Roosevelt's first task as leader of the Rough Riders was to get them moving again toward Santiago. On the morning of June 30, 1898, he ordered 490 soldiers to pack a canteen full of water and three days' worth of rations. About 6,000 regular Army soldiers also prepared to advance toward the city.

On July 1, as they marched toward Santiago, the regiments came under attack. On a road between two hills, Spanish soldiers fired down on them. Roosevelt's troops were caught in a terrible crossfire, and most of them scrambled to take cover. Captain Buckey O'Neill stood in the open, trying to organize his men. One shouted, "Captain, get down! A bullet is sure to hit you!" O'Neill defiantly answered that no Spanish bullet could kill him. Not long after, a bullet struck him in the head and took his life.

The Rough Riders proceeded to Kettle Hill on their

In the Trenches, *a painting of the Battle of Santiago in the Spanish-American War*

right. Roosevelt led the way on horseback. Running and crouching low to avoid Spanish bullets, the Rough Riders made their way up the hill. Roosevelt dismounted from his horse and joined the assault on foot. Bit by bit, they pushed the Spanish troops back. Roosevelt was one of the first U.S. soldiers to reach the top of the hill.

The soldiers began celebrating, but they were still under fire. Now, bullets were coming from San Juan Hill, a higher peak a short distance away. Roosevelt knew his soldiers would have to make another assault. He led them forward on the charge that would make them famous. Bullets flew from the top of the hill, but the Rough Riders kept up the fight.

They moved forward in a zigzag fashion. Several times, they stopped to take cover behind boulders and in trenches. Finally, the Spanish saw the wave of blue-shirted

Frederic Remington's painting, The Charge of the Rough Riders, *1898*

35

soldiers coming toward them. They fled the hill and retreated to the city of Santiago. Roosevelt's Rough Riders and the regular Army units quickly swarmed over the top of San Juan Hill.

The Battle of San Juan Hill did not take long, but it became one of the most famous military actions in American

The U.S. Army celebrates its victory after storming San Juan Hill on July 1, 1898.

Many American soldiers were buried in Cuba during the Spanish-American War.

history. The U.S. Army now had control of the high
ground surrounding Santiago. Victory had come at a high
price, however. Thirteen Rough Riders were killed, and
another 76 were wounded. During their time in Cuba, the
Rough Riders suffered more deaths than any other Army
unit of their size. The regiment lost 25 men in battle and
19 from disease.

Within weeks, the Spanish at Santiago surrendered
to the U.S. Army. Other Spanish forces in Puerto Rico
and the Philippine Islands also surrendered. It was a
sweeping U.S. victory. Spain lost control of Cuba and
gave up Puerto Rico and Guam to the United States. The

United States paid $20 million for control of the Philippines. After that, the United States became an international power and began to play a greater role in world affairs.

Roosevelt was proud of his regiment. He wrote, "Nothing can take away the fact that ... I commanded the regiment and led it victoriously in a hard-fought battle. San Juan was the great day of my life."

American troops receive news of the Spanish army's surrender at Santiago, Cuba, 1898.

AFTER THE WAR

Roosevelt worked hard to get his Rough Riders home. Like other officers, he was concerned that many of his soldiers would fall ill with malaria or yellow fever. Their camps were unsanitary, and the troops were getting sick.

The Rough Riders gather at Camp Wycoff on Long Island, New York, upon their return from the Spanish-American War in Cuba.

William McKinley, U.S. president from 1897-1901

Theodore Roosevelt became president of the United States when McKinley was assassinated.

40

More soldiers died of disease than in combat during the Spanish-American War.

After serving their country four months, the Rough Riders returned to the United States. Their volunteer service was over. They turned in their rifles, equipment, and horses. The men shook hands, said good-bye, and went home. Roosevelt remembered them as "a regiment of as gallant fighters as ever wore the United States uniform." To the American people, they were heroes.

The accomplishments of the Rough Riders made Roosevelt even more famous. He became a nearly unstoppable force in American politics. In 1900, he was elected vice president under President McKinley. When McKinley was assassinated in 1901, Roosevelt took over as president of the United States and served until 1909.

The Rough Riders' short term of duty was over, but they would meet again. Six hundred of them celebrated their first reunion in 1899. They gathered for many more reunions throughout the 1900s. The nation and the world would remember the Rough Riders. As Roosevelt said, "I will talk about the regiment forever."

The Rough Riders posed for a photo in the spot where they had charged over San Juan Hill. **41**

GLOSSARY

assassinated—murdered, often for political reasons

canteen—a small metal container for holding water

cavalry—an army unit on horseback

crossfire—gunfire coming from more than one place

immigrant—a person who moves from one country to live permanently in another

leggings—a protective covering that is wrapped around the lower leg

malaria—a disease that causes fever and chills; it is spread by the bite of mosquitoes that carry the disease

manifest destiny—the term used to describe the belief that the United States should expand its territories

mine—an explosive device that is concealed underground or underwater

rations—food given to soldiers each day

rebels—people who fight against a government or ruler

recruiting—signing up new members of a military force

regiment—a military group made up of about 1,000 soldiers

slouch hat—a wide-brimmed felt hat with a chin strap and one side of the brim turned up, worn as part of a military uniform

yellow fever—a viral disease that is spread by the bite of mosquitoes that carry the disease

DID YOU KNOW?

- The last of the Rough Riders was Jesse Langdon, who died in 1975.

- Disease was the most deadly enemy of U.S. soldiers in the Spanish-American War. More than 5,000 soldiers died of yellow fever and other diseases during the war.

- In 1906, President Theodore Roosevelt was awarded the Nobel Peace Prize.

- In 2001, 82 years after Theodore Roosevelt's death, he was awarded the Medal of Honor for bravery in the Battle of San Juan Hill.

- In 1912, the U.S. Navy pulled the wreckage of the USS *Maine* from Havana Harbor in Cuba. It was taken to deep waters north of Havana and sunk.

- In 1959, Cuba became a communist nation, headed by Fidel Castro.

IMPORTANT DATES

Timeline

1858 Theodore Roosevelt is born in New York City on October 27.

1897 Roosevelt is appointed assistant secretary of the U.S. Navy.

1898 USS *Maine* explodes in Havana Harbor on February 15.

U.S. Congress declares war on Spain on April 21.

1st United States Volunteer Cavalry (the Rough Riders) gathers at Camp Wood in Texas for training in May.

The Rough Riders arrive in Cuba June 22.

Roosevelt leads the Rough Riders and other troops in successful assault of Kettle Hill and San Juan Hill on July 1.

Spanish troops surrender on July 17.

Treaty of Paris is signed on December 10, bringing an official end to the Spanish-American War.

1901 Roosevelt becomes president of the United States on September 14.

IMPORTANT PEOPLE

RUSSELL ALGER (1836–1907)
Secretary of war for the United States from 1897 to 1899; offered the command of the 1st United States Volunteer Cavalry (the Rough Riders) to Theodore Roosevelt

WILLIAM MCKINLEY (1843–1901)
President of the United States during the Spanish-American War

WILLIAM OWEN "BUCKEY" O'NEILL (1860–1898)
Former Arizona sheriff who became a captain in the 1st United States Volunteer Cavalry (the Rough Riders); was killed in action in Cuba on July 1, 1898

THEODORE ROOSEVELT (1858–1919)
Colonel of the 1st United States Volunteer Cavalry (the Rough Riders) who led the charge up San Juan Hill in Cuba; became the 26th president of the United States in 1901

LEONARD WOOD (1860–1927)
The first commander of the 1st United States Volunteer Cavalry (the Rough Riders); he became Army chief of staff under President William Howard Taft

WANT TO KNOW MORE?

At the Library

Collins, Mary. *The Spanish-American War.* New York: Children's Press, 1997.

Green, Robert. *Theodore Roosevelt.* Minneapolis: Compass Point Books, 2003.

Roosevelt, Theodore. *The Rough Riders.* Dallas: Taylor Publishing, 1997.

On the Web

For more information on *Roosevelt's Rough Riders,* use

FactHound to track down Web sites related to this book.

1. Go to *www.facthound.com.*

2. Type in a search word related to this book
   or this book ID: 0756512689.

3. Click on the *Fetch It* button.

Your trusty FactHound will fetch the best Web sites for you!

On the Road

Theodore Roosevelt Birthplace National Historic Site

28 E. 20th St.

New York, NY 10003

212/260-1616

To visit the place where Theodore Roosevelt was born and lived until he was 14 years old

Sagamore Hill National Historic Site

20 Sagamore Hill Road

Oyster Bay, NY 11771

516/922-4788

To visit the home of Theodore Roosevelt from 1885 until his death in 1919

Look for more We the People books about this era:

Angel Island

The Great Chicago Fire

Great Women of the Suffrage Movement

The Harlem Renaissance

The Haymarket Square Tragedy

The Hindenburg

Industrial America

The Johnstown Flood

The Lowell Mill Girls

A complete list of We the People titles is available on our Web site: *www.compasspointbooks.com*

INDEX

About the Author

Andrew Santella writes for magazines and newspapers, including *GQ* and the *New York Times Book Review*. He is the author of a number of books for young readers. He lives outside Chicago with his wife and son.